A Cup of Sun

By Joan Walsh Anglund

A Cup of Sun

A
Book
of
Poems
by
Joan Walsh Anglund

Harcourt, Brace & World, Inc., New York

B.9.67
Library of Congress Catalog Card Number: 67-24870
Printed in the United States of America

To a very dear and special friend

One seed
    can start a garden
One drop
    can start a sea
One doubt
    can start a hating
One dream
    can set us free.

I have bravery
        to spend on pain
I have faith
        to wall up fear
I have courage
        to fight danger when it comes.
But there is no defense against loneliness.

Beauty
is
my
only
candle
    against
        the
        midnight
            of
            my
            fear.

A bird does not sing
    because he has an answer.

He sings
    because he has a song.

Like all good teachers,
    the world repeats her lesson.
Over and over
                ...with wordless variety...
    she spells the name of Love.

Every tear
    I ever cried
Turned to pearl
    before it died.

Every pain
    that in me burned
Forged to wisdom
    I had earned.

A cup of sun…

 a daisy…

 a thimbleful of snow…

 a leaf turned red from frost's first touch…

this much of God I know.

Thoughts,
    rest your wings.
Here is
    a hollow of silence,
a nest of stillness
    in which to hatch your dreams.

The arabesques a hope can do...
    the dances dreams can make...
the patterned pain a mind may shape...
    before a heart will break.

Day!
  Now thoughts begin.

On dawn's gray back
  old fears ride in.

What can this Spring say
    that other Springs have not already told us?

And yet, each year, how happily we listen!

Faith is the patient seamstress
    who mends our torn belief,
who sews the hem of childhood trust
    and clips the threads of grief.

Why, when others were winged,
was I made snail…
to crawl on humblest garden path,
to leave such slender trail?

There is only one doorway
into Forever...
and Death keeps the only key.

Success is a garden
with too much sun.

Be careful it does not dry your roots.

The ugly face of fear
    stares behind the masks of many faces.
I watch it in the crowds,
    I glimpse it in the city.
And often…at home…
    it waits within the mirror.

Be still…

        and let the wind speak.

Hush…

        a world is talking.

Like a great dark bird,

                    winging home,

Tragedy

        drops into the waiting nest,
     woven by our weaknesses.

To put a seed
        in the earth
    is to be a mother.

To feed a bird
        on snowy days
    is to be a host to God.

Loneliness speaks to loneliness.
And though we mask ourselves
with words or silences,
our needs leap out from all we do
and speak to those alike.

Self-importance
        sits in the back seat,
    and directs all our travels.

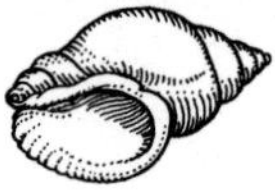

Just outside my wisdom
   are words that would answer everything.

A thimble over Caring
     to keep the aching out...
Such armor should the heart wear
     whenever Love's about.

Sleep is a small death...
　　yet we do not fear it.

Sleep is a small death....
　　Does it tell us of a larger dream?

I shall be older than this
    one day.
I shall think myself young
    when I remember.
Nothing can stop
    the slow change of masks my face must wear,
    one following one.
These gloves my hands have put on,
    the pleated skin, patterned by
    the pale tracings of my days...
These are not *my* hands!
    And yet, these gloves do not come off!
I shall wear older ones tomorrow,
    till, glove after glove,
    and mask after mask,
    I am buried beneath
    the baggage of Old Woman.
Oh, then,
    shall I drop them off,
Unbutton the sagging, misshapen apparel of age,
    and run, young and naked, into Eternity!

I did not hear
    the words you said.

Instead,
    I heard the love.

What *is* poetry,
　　if it is not the silent singing
　　　each man hears
　　　　within his own heart?